GET THEM TO BUY INTO YOU

The Student Guide To Personal And Professional Success

Treandos Thornton

Published by Al Duncan Publishing LLC

www.alduncanpublishing.com

Copyright © 2011 Treandos Thornton

All rights reserved. No part of this publication may be reproduced, stored in a retrieval system or transmitted in any form or by any means, electronic, mechanical, photocopying, scanning, or otherwise, without the written permission of the author.

ISBN13:978-0-9831900-3-5

Cover Design by SS Media

I want to send a special thanks to my unborn son, wife, mom and dad for all of the sacrifices you made.

Treandos Lisco Thornton

Shana Thomas-Thornton

Peggy J. Thornton

Sammie L. Thornton

Contents

Introduction vii
Chapter 1: I Will Persist 1
Chapter 2: Why People Buy 7
Chapter 3: Like You 11
Chapter 4: Feel, Felt, Found 19
Chapter 5: Know You 23
Chapter 6: Types of Stories 24
Chapter 7: Appearance 32
Chapter 8: Elevator Pitch 37
Chapter 9: Trust You 42
Chapter 10: Four Personalities 45
Chapter 11: Interviewing Skills 55
Chapter 12: Resume Information 79
Chapter 13: Top Questions 83
Chapter 14: Conclusion 102

Introduction – Why I Wrote This Book

I wrote this book because I want to make YOU more successful in your career! I want to help make you more confident when meeting absolute strangers! I want to ensure people remember you as a distinct individual!

I want to teach you practical skills that will help you negotiate any demanding situation, such as a networking scenario, a professional job or internship interview, or simply an initial meeting with new individuals. I'm quite certain that if you apply these critical skills you'll likely establish instant rapport.

The most important reason I wrote this book is so that you could win in any situation! I define winning in simple terms: get people to buy into you! Period!

Let's get started!

"You are the most important common denominator when it comes to people buying into you."

Let's face it: the marketplace is so competitive when it comes to getting a job, getting an internship, and when trying to differentiate yourself during a networking opportunity, that the task can seem quite daunting. So, to help you build the confidence to meet that challenge, we're going to take our first step. We're going to look at what we'll call, simply, "you." The only thing that's different from everyone else is you. Your unique skills, looks, knowledge and expertise together are what's going to separate you from all the others, and get people to **buy into you.** You must remember that out of the billions of humans that have been alive, there's no one like you.

When meeting anyone for the very first time, you only have about 10 to 15 seconds to get people to buy the concept of you. **A wise man once said, "Your first impression is your only impression."** Like it or not, if you don't connect during the first 10 to 15 seconds, you can forget the rest of the process. I'm sure you can recall a time when you met a stranger for the first time, and you thought "I can't stand this person!" There are many possible reasons why you felt that way, but it's quite likely your particular reason came within the first 10 to 15 seconds of the encounter.

In this book you will learn how to become more effective during any initial conversation. Once you move past the initial obstacles, you will be on your way to becoming a master of getting other people to buy into you. There are reasons why people buy you, and the first reason is because it is clear that you have bought into yourself. The second reason is, they like you and the third reason is that they trust you.

There is a success road map to getting people to buy you, and it consists of getting people to know you, like you, and finally, to trust you.

Chapter 1

I Will Persist

People want to know more about you when you have things in common. If you're from the same city, like the same teams, or come from the same background, you typically will have a connection. Just the other day, I was getting out of a meeting and introduced myself to a stranger in the room. I asked the person where he was from, and he happened to be from the same city I'm from, so we had an instant connection. We talked a little bit more and found out that we knew some of the same people. Before I knew it, we'd been talking for about 10 minutes. Conversations like this are what you're trying to create in each situation. A couple of years ago, I wouldn't have been able to engage in a conversation of this sort. If I could travel back in the past and compare myself to who I am now, there would be no comparison.

It all started for me several years ago, after I graduated from college. I needed a job, so I took a sales job where I was selling business and home loans over the phone. In order to for me to get more leads outside of my non-existent network, I would have to go out and meet new people. The very thought of me talking to strange people for the first time had me scared straight. In order to conquer this fear, I decided that I would go to a few networking events. The first time that I attended a networking event, I forgot my business cards!

So, make sure that you have some form of a business card with you at all times. A business card is the best way to stay in contact with people you meet. Once you have their card, make sure that you write down something about that person so you can easily remember what you discussed. For example, if you meet someone at a networking event or meeting, and you chat about a specific football team, you want to write this information down, so the next time you talk to that person, you'll remember that you already have a common ground to discuss. Caution: Make sure you don't write on the person's business card in front of them. This can seem offensive and just downright rude. You should always keep a note pad handy, or type the information into your cell phone. After attending that event without my business cards, I decided that I would always carry cards on me at all times.

I can still recall feeling nauseous as I picked up the telephone to make my very first sales call. I was sweating bullets as I stumbled over my sales pitch. Needless to say, the defiant customer hung up on me! After that infamous initial sales call, the selling did get easier for me. After several months on the job, I was able to successfully deal with customers' concerns. I truly listened to my customers. I addressed their needs. I do acknowledge that belief and confidence encouraged me to pick up the telephone and persuade complete strangers to buy the product and service. Selling is truly one of the most valuable skills needed for personal and professional success! This job taught me all of these principles that I'm going to talk about in this book.

Chapter 1: I Will Persist

What's the difference between a two-year-old child and a teenager?

Answer: The child is more persistent, and continues to ask for whatever they want. The teenager will ask for what they want approximately two times, while the two year old child will go on asking. The child does not understand the word no. A child has all of the necessary skills to get people to buy into him or her, which is to continue to ask until…..

In life, most of the most successful people learn that if you want to succeed, you have to fail your way to the top. Below is one of my favorite poems; I live by it:

I Will Persist Until I Succeed
By Og Mandino

In the Orient young bulls are tested for the fight arena in a certain manner. Each is brought to the ring and allowed to attack a picador, who pricks them with a lance. The bravery of each bull is then rated with care according to the number of times he demonstrates his willingness to charge in spite of the sting of the blade. Henceforth will I recognize that each day I am tested by life in like manner. If I persist, if I continue to try, if I continue to charge forward, I will succeed.

I will persist until I succeed.

I was not delivered unto this world in defeat, nor does failure course in my veins. I am not a sheep waiting to be prodded by my shepherd. I am a lion and I refuse to talk, to walk, to sleep with the sheep. I will hear not those who weep and complain, for their disease is contagious. Let them join the sheep. The slaughterhouse of failure is not my destiny.

I will persist until I succeed.

The prizes of life are at the end of each journey, not near the beginning; and it is not given to me to know how many steps are necessary in order to reach my goal. Failure I may still encounter at the thousandth step, yet success hides behind the next bend in the road. Never will I know how close it lies unless I turn the corner.

Always will I take another step. If that is of not available I will take another, and yet another. In truth, one step at a time is not too difficult.

I will persist until I succeed.

Henceforth, I will consider each day's effort as but one blow of my blade against a mighty oak. The first blow may cause not a tremor in the wood, nor the second, nor the third. Each blow, of itself, may be trifling and seem of no consequence. Yet from childish swipes the oak will eventually tumble. So it will be with my efforts of today.

I will be liken to the rain drop which washes away the mountain; the ant who devours a tiger; the star which brightens the earth; the slave who builds a pyramid. I will build my castle one brick at a time for I know that small attempts, repeated, will complete any undertaking.

I will persist until I succeed.

I will never consider defeat and I will remove from my vocabulary such words and phrases as quit, cannot, unable, impossible, out of the question, improbable, failure, unworkable, hopeless and retreat; for they are the words of fools. I will avoid despair but if this disease of the mind should infect me then I will work on in despair. I will toil and I will endure. I will ignore the obstacles at my feet and keep mine eyes on the goals above my head, for I know that where dry desert ends, green grass grows.

I will persist until I succeed.

I will remember the ancient law of averages and I will bend it to my good. I will persist with knowledge that each failure to sell will increase my chance for success at the next attempt. Each nay I hear will bring me closer to the sound of yea. Each frown I meet only prepares me for the smile to come. Each misfortune I encounter will carry in it the seed of tomorrow's good luck. I must have the night to appreciate the day. I must fail often to succeed only once.

I will persist until I succeed.

I will try, and try, and try again. Each obstacle I will consider as a mere detour to my goal and a challenge to my profession. I will persist and develop my skills as the mariner develops his, by learning to ride out the wrath of each storm.

I will persist until I succeed.

Henceforth, I will learn and apply another secret of those who excel in my work. When each day is ended, not regarding whether it has been a success or failure, I will attempt to achieve one more sale. When my thoughts beckon my tired body homeward I will resist the temptation to depart. I will try again. I will make one more attempt to close with victory, and if that fails I will make another. Never will I allow any day to end in failure. Thus will I plant the seed of tomorrow's success and gain an insurmountable advantage over those who cease their labor at a prescribed time. When others cease their struggle, then mine will begin, and my harvest will be full.

I will persist until I succeed.

Nor will I allow yesterday's success to lull me into today's complacency, for this is the great foundation of failure. I will forget the happenings of the day that is gone, whether they were good or bad, and greet the new sun with confidence that this will be the best day of my life.

So long as there is breath in me, that long will I persist. For now I know one of the greatest principles of success; if I persist long enough I will win.

I will persist.

I will win.

Chapter 2

Why People Buy

"Life is a Sale. And the path to success at both living and selling is the same"

Most people hate selling, or even the idea of it. As a child, you are programmed by your friends, parents, and teachers to dislike Selling. Your parents told you that most salespeople are con artists. Movies like Two for the Money and Boiler Room portray salespeople as dishonest, pushy, and rude. Let's focus on the truth, and the truth is that from your birth you have always selling. Beginning in your early childhood, you made a lot of sales calls. You worked your sales magic on your parents for them to take you to Six Flags or Disney World. When your parents told you to go to bed at a certain time, you worked your sales skills to get a 30 minute extension. You gave them a sales pitch to have a friend sleep over. If you received a poor grade in school, you sold your parents on the fact that it was not your fault. Whether you like it or not, your childhood prepared you for adulthood. When you went to the car dealership for the first time, you tried to talk the salesperson down to a lower price. In reality you were not selling, you were just getting people to buy into you.

There are really three reasons why people buy into you. In order for someone to buy into you they must like you. The second reason is, they must know you. The final reason is, they must trust you. Let's talk a little more about people liking you. When it comes to people liking you, many factors come into play. The way you look, the way you dress, the way you talk, and your attractiveness or unattractiveness will have a huge effect on whether or not someone will like you. For example, if you take two individuals that have never met, and they find out that they know some of the same people from the same city; they will have a common ground.

Here are six statements about getting people to buy into you that you should understand:

1. Getting people to buy into you opens the door for opportunity

2. Sales is considered an exchange of values

3. Selling is not what you do to someone, it's something you do for people

4. If you can get people to know you, like you, and trust you, then they will be sold on you

5. Closing is victorious when you and the customer win.

6. Develop trust and rapport before you begin the process of selling

I can still remember the first time that I got someone to buy into me. It happened when I was in second grade. My math teacher said that whoever could get the most people to buy the candy bars could win a Walkman. (I know most kids now have never heard or have never seen a Walkman.) As soon as she said that, I told myself that I had to win that Walkman. Losing this contest was not going to happen to me. Who would want to buy the candy bars from me was the first question. How was I going to get in front of the people that would buy the candy bars was my next question. After thinking about these questions for a long time, I decided that it was time for me to get my parents to help me.

So, I sat down with my parents and explained that I needed their help if I was going to win. They agreed to help under certain circumstances. It's amazing, when you think about it, that you have been trying to get people to buy into you since birth. As a baby you cried, banged your hands on the table when you wanted people to feed you or change your diaper. When you got a few years older you would ask your parents repeatedly for what you wanted. Can you remember being in the toy store with your mother? Begging her for that toy? Even if your parents initially told you know in the beginning, you continued to ask until they said yes. That's what you call being persistent.

Sometimes you will have to be persistent in order for someone to buy into you. You must live by the quote "I will persist until I succeed." For example, most children learn how to walk after falling down thousands of times. What if children were to stop trying? Well, thousands of humans would never learn how to walk, run, and stand up. This principle is no different from getting people to buy into you.

Can you remember trying to get a date in high school and college? That was getting someone to buy into you. They bought into your looks, and your conversation. Whether you like it or not, getting people to buy into you is the same as selling. When you asked your girl friend or boy friend to go to the movies with you, that was selling. If you can get the other person to see everything from your perspective, you have got them to buy into you. People only buy into you for three reasons. The first reason that someone buys into you is because they know you. The second reason is that they like you.

The third and final reason is that they trust you. You can get to know people through conversations, networking, questions, sharing personal stories. Steven Covey said it best, in The Seven Habits of Highly Effective People: **"Seek first to understand, to be understood."** You probably can remember a time when you met a new person and began to engage in a conversation for the first time, and it just felt like you'd known that person your entire life. During this conversation, both parties talked about something that interested each person. This is called a connection point. For example, let's say you're talking to someone who's lived in the same city as you have. You both have a common ground to talk about, such as restaurants, schools, and maybe hangout spots. Connection is one of the most powerful components in an initial meeting. Either you have it with someone or you don't. It's hard to articulate why you connect with people. This should be one of your top objectives when you're trying to get someone to buy into you.

Chapter 3

Like You

Here a several ways to get people to like you:

1. **Smiling**
2. **Listening**
3. **Use Humor**
4. **Be true to yourself**
5. **Laughter**
6. **Talk in terms of the other's interest**

"The world looks brighter behind a smile."

About six months into my first job as a Salesperson, my manager pulled me to the side. We went into the back office and he closed the door. Usually when someone was asked to go into that office, it was not a good sign. My manager said, "You're doing a great job selling, but there's an area which I think you can work on that could make you get even better." My first thought was to object to what he was saying, but I decided to listen to him. He began to tell me that he thought that I didn't smile enough when I was on the phone selling, and in person. He said to try and smile when you're talking to customers on the phone and in person. I immediately put those tips into play and, lo and behold, my sales actually increased. What I noticed was that when I smiled while on the phone and in person, I felt at ease. My customers seemed to have nicer responses.

Now, this principle doesn't help in every situation, because some people are just not going to buy into you. A study by the Gallup group has shown that if you smile at people when you pass them, 3 out of 4 people will smile back. When I read this, I didn't believe it was true. So I decided to try it myself, and I found out that it worked. Most people will smile back. It also seems to make people feel better. When you smile at the angriest-looking people, their eyes seem to brighten right up. A study conducted by the British Dental Health Foundation showed the act of smiling to dramatically improve one's mood. Dr. Nigel Carter, the foundation's CEO, stated: "We have long been drawing attention to the fact that smiling increases happiness both in yourself and those around you, so it is good to receive the backing of this scientific research. A healthy smile can improve your confidence, help you make friends and help you to succeed in your career."

As for me, if it makes someone else's day a little brighter, then I will keep smiling.

Smiling has even been related to having better health. A good smile can brighten the room. Studies have shown that people who smile more seem be more attractive than those who don't (Lau, 1982). People who smile more are said to have more control and are at ease. So, the next time you walk into an interview, or walk past someone on your way to work, make sure that you're smiling. Statistics have shown that employers will hire a person who is smiling versus a person who is not smiling.

Laughter

> *"You can't stay mad at somebody who makes you laugh."*
> — Jay Leno

Studies have shown that the average person laughs about 17 times a day. As humans we need to have a good laugh, because it helps to change our mood. The next time that you're about to speak in public, go into a job interview or meet someone new, try and think about something funny. What this will do for you is, it will ease your tension and it will also put you in a better mood. Ask yourself this question: Do you like people who seem to have fun, or people who seem to be upset all the time? If you're like me, you probably like people who enjoy having fun. When you're engaged in a conversation, whether in an interview or with a total stranger, make sure that you use humor. When people laugh with you, they begin to connect with you.

Let's face it; getting people to buy into you is a skill that takes some time to master. The person that has bought into should always feel good about the decision. Have you ever bought something from a salesperson and then walked away feeling upset? If you have felt this way, it was probably because that salesperson violated one of the three principles of knows you, like you, and trust you. You may have felt like you'd been manipulated..

Keep in mind that everyone has a perception of you instantly. Most people make a decision within 5 seconds of whether or not they're going to buy into you. So, you should ask yourself, "What message am I sending out to people?" People perceive you in several ways, such as: body language, appearance, and your vocabulary.

Listening

> "Most of the successful people I've known are the ones who do more listening than talking."

While working at a bank, I was sent to a selling class where I was taught one of the most powerful skills to get people to buy into you: listening. It's one of the most powerful skills that you can use in the selling process. Before learning this skill, if I was trying to persuade someone to buy my product and they said that they couldn't see why it would work, I'd try to show them how it would work. In reality, I was telling the potential client that he was wrong. I was being disrespectful to the client.

Listening can be one of the hardest skills to master during any conversation. We were born with two ears and one mouth. People listen to one radio station: **WIFM** – **W**hat's **I**n **I**t **F**or **M**e. Pay attention to your next three conversations and count how many times the word "I" is used. A good rule to live by is to listen more and talk less. Have you ever noticed that people you enjoy having conversations with tend to listen more?

Listening can help you get people to buy into you by: People tell you in their conversation exactly what they want. For example, if you walked into an interview and asked the interviewer what they were looking for, they would tell you. Here is a four-step process in which you can use the skill of listening to get people to like you:

Step1. Respond by talking about things you agree with the individual on. Make sure to reiterate what you have in common. Always use the words "Yes" and "You're right" to begin your response.

Step2. If someone doesn't agree with you, don't try to prove them wrong. What you should do is, ask yourself what is he or she asking? How can I show them that I have the solutions to their questions?

Step3. When networking, interviewing, and meeting people for the first time, always listen for points you can agree upon. As the person talks, focus on what you have in common.

Step4. Once you have begun to get people to buy into you, then you want to move them to the next steps. Listening to the person's objections and comments gives you the opportunity to address those issues.

Talk about points you agree on:

Great listening can give you a great way to overcome objections and build instant credibility. Try to keep your conversation on specific points of agreement, rather than points of disagreement. When you hear areas of agreement, make a mental note of that information.

Example: Let's say that you are one of the final candidates for a job. So your objective is to get them to buy into you.

> **You:** I'd like to show why I'm the best candidate for the job.
>
> **Prospect:** We already have someone else in mind that seems like a better fit for the job.

Now, you need to accept what the prospect said. Then you want to help the prospect "be right," so he or she can open up to you. The prospect has told you the truth, so it's up to you to convince them otherwise. Once you agree with the prospect, they will be caught off guard.

> **You:** Yes, you probably already have someone else in mind, but as they say, save the best for last. There are three reasons why I feel you should hire me:
>
> Number 1, I'm an individual who comes to work early and leaves late.
>
> Number 2, I have the ability to work well as a member of a team – or to lead the team.
>
> Number 3, I have the ability to communicate with anyone. Is there anything else you need to know before you hire me?

What you have just done is told them three reasons why they should buy you. You also close the prospect out, which is what you always want to do.

Offer Solutions and Next Steps:

Here are some questions you can ask:

What are the next steps for us?

What is the best time for me to follow up with you?

Which one of these options sounds best for you?

Would you like me to follow up by email or a phone call?

Humor: The quality of being amusing or comic, especially as expressed in literature or speech.

Humor can be a great tool to use, but you must handle it with care. Using humor can be a great way to get someone to buy into you. When you get people to smile, they usually are letting down their guard.

Objections:

Sometimes, when you try to get people to buy into you, they will reject you. For example, you are in an interview and you want to close on a strong note. So, you ask the person, "What else do you to need to know before you hire me?" They respond by, saying, "I don't feel like you can get the job done." The interviewer is giving you an objection.

Some common objections are as follows:

I'm not interested

I don't have the time

I don't have enough money

Chapter 4

Feel, Felt, Found

Objections are objects that get in the way of people making a decision, or buying into you. Objections are also signs that the customer – or the person you're talking to – is interested. What an objection actually means is that the project wants more information, clarification, or a simple answer to a question. When most people are confronted with objections, they have no clue how to handle them. Some people will not acknowledge them.

There are several ways you can handle an objection. One of the most popular ways is the "Feel, Felt, and Found" method, which is good for handling quick objections that may come up with during interviews, conversations, or if they're not interested in what you have to offer. The Feel Felt Found technique takes the initial sting out of the objection; use it when confronted with objections that start with "I think," or "I feel."

Here's an example of how you can use the Feel Felt Found method to get someone to buy into you: If someone says that they don't "feel" you're the best candidate, you can reply with: "I can understand why you might **feel** that I'm not the best candidate.

Others have **felt** the same way. However, when they saw my resume and my credentials, they **found** out that I was the best candidate for the job." The best way to get better at using this principle is to practice.

You understand how they feel:

Empathize with the customer. The reason that you use **Feel** is to empathize with the person you're trying to get to buy into you. Tell them that you can understand how they feel as they raise their sales objection. When handling sale objections, you want to work with your customer, not against them. Think of it as a sales martial art technique. You use their force and change the direction, not meet it head-on with another force. The Feel, Felt, Found objection handling technique is a great way of doing that. You're letting them know that it is understandable that they have this objection to the sale. That it's normal, it's happened to other people, and they still ended up buying the product.

Other people felt the same way:

Other customers that bought into me have felt the same way. You are using social proof to show that this is also what others have said, and they went on to buy. Your customer wants to be like others, we all do. Do you enter an empty restaurant? If you see a crowd gathered at a market stall, you go and take a look. If they find it interesting, so could you. Like it or not, we still follow the crowd. Many sales markets rely upon this basic instinct.

"Get in touch with the way the other person feels. Feelings are 55% body language, 38% tone and 7% words."

Chapter 5

Know You

Your body language can be inviting or uninviting. Have you ever noticed that people who smile often seem to be friendlier than people who frown? People who smile more seem more approachable. Your state of mind has a lot to do with your body language.

Ways to get people to know you:

Your communication skills will either help you or bury you. People first see your appearance, and second, they hear what's coming out of your mouth. In order to improve your communications skill, you can take a Toastmasters class, read books on public speaking, or take a college course. You can record yourself and try to improve the next time. Watching yourself or listening to yourself can be an uncomfortable situation. Have you noticed that the preachers, politicians, attorneys have great communication skills?

Chapter 6

Types of Stories

Facts tell and stories sell:

Have you noticed that most persuasive people tell amazing stories? As a child, you wanted your parents to tell you a bedtime story before you went to sleep. Stories are great ways for you to get know people and for people to get to know you. Stories have an introduction, a body and a conclusion. **There are six types of stories that you can tell:**

1. The first type of story is <u>I know what you are thinking story</u>. Stories that make people wonder if you're reading their minds are amazing to them. If you've done some homework on the person or group that you want to buy into you, it will be easy to identify their objections.

2. The second type of story is called a <u>vision story</u>. It lets the other person know exactly what your values, morals, and beliefs are. Martin Luther King's I Have a Dream speech is a good example of a vision story.

Vision stories, if told truthfully, can sometimes get you a standing ovation. If you get a standing ovation while delivering a vision story, you have just guaranteed that they have bought into you. But you must use good sense and make sure your vision story is appropriate for your target audience, because a vision story can, and sometimes will be taken out of context. A president of a multimillion dollar company told his employees a story about wanting to take the company from a $5 million a year business to a $10 million a year one. The problem with this story is that most employees are generally not moved to double the income of the company they work for.

3. The third type of story that you can use to get people to buy into you is a <u>teaching story</u>. Telling a student about what they should say to get someone to buy into them may work. A more effective way would be to tell a story of an intelligent student getting someone to buy into them during a job interview or an internship after being asked a question.

   Whenever I speak to an audience, I always try to teach them certain skills. This can be a challenging feat sometimes. A lot of people would get very upset in this situation. I find that the best way to teach people how to do something is by using a teaching story.

4. The fourth type of story to use to get people to buy into you is a <u>value in action story</u>. One of the best ways to tell a value in action story is to give an example. I remember one day when I was headed to the cleaners to

pick up my clothes. On the way, I realized that I didn't have any cash on me. So I headed to the nearest drive-through ATM. As I pulled up to the ATM machine, the person in front of me finished his transaction and drove off fast, forgetting to get his card out of the machine. I immediately felt sorry for him, so I drove off and tried to see if I could catch him. As I was passing a gas station, I spotted the driver of the white truck who'd left his debit card behind. I walked up to the gentlemen and said, "Sir, you left this at the ATM." He stared and looked baffled, and finally said, "Thanks."

This story illustrates my values without having to spell them out. Through that story you find out that I have good morals, I'm trustworthy, and I'm willing to go out of my way to help a complete stranger. Telling value in action stories is the best way to get people to buy into you. A good test for you would be to see how many personal values in action stories you can come up with, and then be sure to write them down for future use.

5. The fifth type of story that you can tell to get someone to buy into you is a <u>why I am here story</u>. Most people won't buy into you if they think you're not trustworthy or crooked. People want to feel that you have their best interests at heart early on. If you're communicating to an audience, they will want to know what's in it for them. But even before you tell them what's in it for them, you might need to tell them what's in it for you! For example, if I want you to buy a product or service from me, you probably would like to know what I will get out of the situation first.

Can you remember ever going into your local grocery store and seeing the Girl Scouts standing outside, selling their cookies? You'd more than likely purchase some of the cookies, because you know that your money would go to a worthy cause. The second reason is because they're good cookies. Everyone knows why the Girl Scouts are in front of the local grocery store selling cookies.

A <u>why I am here story</u> often displays dishonesty or some type of ambition. I remember once speaking with a successful business owner who shared with me the story that he would tell people during his presentation. He was from Haiti and had come to the United States with no knowledge of English and only a few dollars in his pocket. He started out working in a dish room of a restaurant. Every day he would teach himself a couple words of English by writing them down in his notebook. He would always watch the well-dressed people who came in to the restaurant. He noticed the people who had nice cars and nice families, always wondering if he could have the finer things in life. He eventually learned English, and went on to start several successful businesses. Once investors, financiers and other people hear the story, they automatically buy into him– even though his story clearly displays goals that are self-centered. People are OK that he's being honest.

6. The sixth type of story that you can tell is a <u>who I am story</u>. One of the first things people ask themselves once they figure out that you want them to buy into you is, "Who is this guy?" Remember that people buy into you

only because they know you, like you, and trust you. So you want the audience to like who you are initially. If you are in front of an audience you can start out with a joke or tell a compelling story about yourself.

What is the most important thing when it comes to getting people to buy into you? Is it your resume? Is it your knowledge of the company? Is it your fancy business card that cost you a couple hundred of dollars to create? Well, I could continue to ask questions for days, but the bottom line is that none of those guesses is correct. Do some of those things matter? Yes, but they are only the beginning. At the end of the day people only buy you. Remember that people buy into you only because they know you, like you, and trust you.

Your most powerful asset is not your resume, nor your appearance. Rather, it's something you see every single day in the mirror. That person is you! Getting people to buy into you is not a hard thing to do. It all starts with getting people to know you. Then you have to get them to like you, and then, finally, to trust you. Once people like you, then you can focus on building trust by listening and asking good questions. If you take the time to listen to people, they truly feel like you care about their needs. Keep in mind that people love to hear compliments, stories, and information that relates to their lives. **Here are five tips on how to improve your story-telling skills.**

1. Know your material. You can't be a great storyteller unless you have something worthwhile to say.

2. Be yourself. Put your story into your own words.

3. Don't spew everything you know: Make your stories follow a basic structure.

4. Assess your audience as you speak. Watch for their reactions and adjust accordingly.

5. Sometimes giving less information is better than too much. Allow for conversation to occur (come up for air).

Before you can get people to buy into you, you must first buy into yourself. If you look up the word *buy* in the dictionary, you'll find it means "to accept as true." In order to buy into yourself you must accept the truth about yourself. Knowing the truth about yourself begins when you start to believe in yourself. In the movie The Matrix, Neo is supposed to be the chosen one. As the story of the Matrix goes on, Neo takes the red pill and begins to live outside of the Matrix. Morpheus is the only one who believes that he is the one. The biggest problem is that Neo does not believe in himself. As the movie progresses, Neo's self-belief is challenged in a fight scene, in which Neo is losing at the beginning, but he gets better and better as he continues. By the second movie, Neo begins to fly and is able to stand up to Agent Smith. In the final Matrix, Neo totally believes he is the one.

In order for you to believe in yourself, you're going to have to try new things. You might fail at some of them initially, but you'll do better over time. For example, if you go on your first job interview and don't get the job, don't give up, because you will get better in the next interview. The bottom line is that you can only believe in yourself by trying each and every day.

> *"Knowing others is intelligence; knowing yourself is true wisdom. Mastering others is strength; mastering yourself is true power."*

Most people really never get to know themselves.

The first thing that you want to get to know about yourself is your personality. Do you have an outgoing personality, or are you more reserved? Let's take a look at some information that is standard knowledge in the Direct Sales arena. This information has made people millions upon millions of dollars in that arena.

"The individual who asks the questions controls the outcome."

If you're skilled at asking questions, then you can find out exactly what you need to know. For example, when you go to the doctor, what's the first thing he says to you? He asks you questions to find out what's wrong. The reason he does that is to try and pinpoint what you're suffering from. If doctors didn't do this but instead simply assumed what your problem is and prescribed whatever medicine came to mind, millions of people would die.

You can also get to know yourself by asking questions. You can ask yourself: "What's the most important thing about XYX?" The next question is, "How do I know when I have that?" The third and final question is, "Is there anything more important than that?" You can ask yourself this set of questions in any area of your life. I used these questions to help a young man who was in the audience of one of my speaking engagements. He was trying to decide whether to take a certain job.

What is the most important thing to me about a job?
Answer: Be able to make good money.

How do you know when you're making good money?
Answer: When I'm making enough money to pay my bills and still saving money.

Is there anything more important than that?
Answer: I want a job that I love to do.

How do you know when you love your job?
Answer: When I wake up in the morning and can't wait to get to work.

Is there anything more important than that?
Answer: No

> *"Getting someone to like you is merely the other side of your liking them."*
>
> *— Normal Vincent Peale*

Chapter 7

Appearance

Getting someone to like you can be a hit or miss scenario. It is almost impossible to build rapport if someone does not like you. According to Harvard Business School, it takes an individual approximately 3 seconds before they judge whether or not they like you. There are several factors which contribute to someone liking you. Your appearance, body language, eye contact, communication skills, rapport and your attitude are all contributing factors of whether or not someone likes you.

How important is wearing the proper attire to an interview? Let's say that you have an interview for a sales job. For this interview you can choose to wear a shirt and tie, or you can wear a suit. Which outfit do you think will be best for this scenario? Hopefully, you chose the full suit. It is always best to wear a suit to an interview instead of a shirt and tie. A dark two piece suit and a dark tie would be the combination to wear to an interview. Don't forget to wear a nice pair of wing-tip dress shoes that are polished. Dressing too flashy for an interview can immediately make the interviewer not like you. If in doubt about what to wear, remember that a man should always wear a suit jacket and a tie

Chapter 7: Appearance

to an interview. Women should wear a professional suit or dress and a pair of low- heeled shoes. You should make sure that your clothes are cleaned, pressed, and fitted. If you have gained or lost weight, you want to make sure your clothes fit well. Remember that a person makes their decisions on whether or not they like you within 3 seconds, so you want to dress to impress.

Russell Simmons said it best: **"Your first impression could be your last impression."**

Your haircut and facial hair are also components of your appearance. Going to an interview with unshaved facial hair and no haircut shows an employer that you don't care. I can remember when I had just graduated from college, and I had an interview with one of the largest banks in the South. I didn't own a suit at the time. I decided to go to the interview with a sports coat and khakis. That was a funny mistake.

I can still remember that when I walked in to the interview the interviewer's eyes lit up. I thought that was going to be a good sign for me, but unfortunately it was not. Of course, I didn't get the job. Looking back on that interview, I think my appearance was the main reason that I did not get the job. You have to look in the mirror and ask yourself, would I hire this person if I was the one doing the interviewing? If you answer yes, good job. If you answer no, you have some work to do. If you don't buy into yourself when you look in the mirror, then the person interviewing you won't, either.

Here is how you tie a bowtie:

To tie the Bow Tie Knot, select a bow tie of your choice and stand in front of a mirror. Then simply follow the steps below:

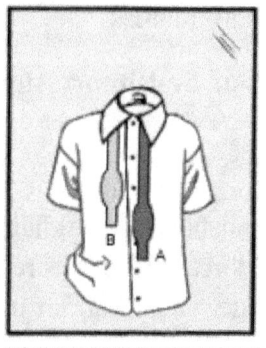

1) Place the bow tie around your neck, situating it so that end "A" is about two inches longer than end "B".

2) Cross end "A" over end "B".

3) Bring end "A" up and under the loop.

Chapter 7: Appearance 35

4) Now double end "B" over itself to form the front base loop of the bow tie.

5) Loop end "A" over the center of the loop you just formed.

6) Holding everything in place, double end "A" back on itself and poke it through the loop behind the bow tie.

7) Adjust the bow tie by tugging at the ends of it and straightening the center knot.

> *"Fifty five percent of communication is body language."*
>
> — *Tony Robbins*

Have you noticed that most of the nicest people smile a lot? That should be a clue to you that if you're going to get someone to buy into you, you should smile. People who smile seem more inviting and friendlier. Have you ever met someone and noticed that they never gave you direct eye contact? When you are meeting someone for the first time, looking them in the eye or avoiding eye contact can send an instant message. Looking people in the eye during your introduction will let them know you have respect for them. Human beings are drawn to people who have high self esteem. If someone doesn't make eye contact, you tend to think that they have self esteem issues. Eye contact gives you credibility, and is an important element in the establishment and development of a relationship.

Learning to understand this form of nonverbal communication can help you make a good first impression and aid you in decoding the messages others are trying to send – whether they are gazing into your eyes or actively avoiding them. According to researchers, people who have great eye contact tend to have the most friends. Tip: Make more eye contact.

Chapter 8

Elevator Pitch

An Elevator Pitch is a 15 second statement which describes you, what you do, and how you do it; it's a good communication tool, a sales tool that helps you articulate your message. There are several reasons why you should have an elevator pitch: (1) It helps you create an interest in the product or service you provide. (2) It provides you the opportunity to create a conversation starter. (3) An elevator pitch makes you look professional and knowledgeable about what you have to offer. According to Chris O'Leary, the author of Elevator Pitch Essentials, there are nine C's in an elevator pitch:

1. **Concise**

2. **Clear**

3. **Compelling**

4. **Credible**

5. Conceptual

6. Concrete

7. Customized

8. Consistent

9. Conversational

I discuss each of The Nine C's at length elsewhere, but in the interests of repetition – and one of the themes of this book is that repetition is good – let me give you a quick sense of what I mean.

1. Concise

An effective elevator pitch contains as few words as possible, but no fewer.

2. Clear

Rather than being filled with acronyms, MBA-speak, and ten-dollar words, an effective elevator pitch can be understood by your grandparents, your spouse, and your children.

3. Compelling

An effective elevator pitch explains the problem your Solution solves.

4. Credible

An effective elevator pitch explains why you are qualified to see the problem and to build your Solution.

5. Conceptual

An effective elevator pitch stays at a fairly high level and does not go into too much unnecessary detail.

6. Concrete

As much as is possible, an effective elevator pitch is also specific and tangible.

7. Customized

An effective elevator pitch addresses the specific interests and concerns of the audience.

8. Consistent

Every version of an effective elevator pitch conveys the same basic message.

9. Conversational

The goal of an elevator pitch is not to close the deal, rather it is just to set the hook: to start a conversation, or dialogue, with the audience.

You should always have your elevator pitch ready, because you never know what you're going to run into. For example, I taught this concept about being ready to a group of high school seniors. A few weeks later, one of the students came up to me and told me how it had already come in handy for him. He'd been at a networking event where he used his elevator pitch on a manager who was looking to hire someone.

Chapter 8: Elevator Pitch

Below are some questions that you should think about if you plan to get people to buy into you:

Is it easy for you to make small talk, or do you freeze up?

Do you give firm or hard handshakes?

Do you smile when you meet people?

When speaking with people, do you make eye contact?

How well do you remember the names of the people you meet?

Do you stand upright, or do you slouch over when you stand?

At social gatherings, do you meet new people or hide in the corner?

Do you like to meet new people?

How is your posture while sitting down?

When talking to people, does the conversation flow in a natural way?

Are you a pleasant person to be around?

Chapter 9

Trust You

> *"Whenever you're in conflict with someone, there is one factor that can make the difference between damaging your relationship and deepening it. That factor is attitude."*
>
> — *William James*

A positive attitude can be one of the best characteristics a person can possess. Your attitude is also a contributing factor of whether people buy into you. How will people buy into you if they don't want to know you, because of your attitude? You have the power to control your attitude each and every day. Many people allow outside factors to affect their attitude. When it's raining outside, you'll hear people say it's going to be a horrible day, simply because it's raining. Ask yourself how many people you've met who seemed OK, but they had a bad attitude. Nobody enjoys people who have a bad attitude or negative outlook on everything.

Attitude is defined as a complex mental state involving beliefs and feelings and values and dispositions to act in certain ways. Many times people think that they have an idea what their problems are, but it is their attitude that causes them to handle situations poorly. According to John Maxwell (Developing Leaders Around You), an individual whose attitude causes him or her to handle life in a positive manner is called a "no limit person." These people don't fall prey to the normal limitations of life. He or she is willing to try and achieve their potential. Positive people can go places other people can't go because of their attitude.

At this time, you need to take the time to assess your friends, because they can and will affect your attitude. Hanging around negative people can make you a negative person. On a Friday morning on a red-eye flight, one passenger began to hum. Another passenger sitting next to him, who was upset because of the man's attitude, said "What are you so happy about, it's 6:00 am?" The passenger who was humming said, "This is a day that I've never seen before." Some people become so negative that they can't see the positive in anything. One of the best things that you could do is to stay away from toxic people. People buy you, because of your positive attitude.

We have looked before at the importance of trust in dealing with anyone in any sales, including network marketing. Lack of trust represents about 75% of why people would not deal with someone even if they had a great product or service. In traditional marketing and sales, the best way to build trust is by building rapport. This is the feeling of engagement that people have with the salesperson, or anyone in any situation, really. If we can build huge trust rapidly, the cautious defenses we have about us in any new meeting will drop, and we will hear what is being communicated. Without it, nothing will really get through. In face-to-face encounters there are a number of things people can do to build trust – on a physical level and a psychological level.

The Seven Second Rule

There is an initial summing up people do upon meeting us – the seven second rule of an initial assessment. This is mainly based on our physical appearance and initial words. Once the first impression is formed, it is difficult to change. For the next element of building trust (although, as noted above about how quickly we judge people, it is important that this be incorporated into that initial seven second assessment time) there are two elements. These are in the physical and psychological realms.

Physical Rapport

Physically, we can rapidly build trust by mirroring people. This occurs on a number of levels. General body posture is important, as well as rate and depth of breathing, blink rate, etc. Standing and facing someone does not allow this to be done as effectively as other techniques. For example, being at an angle to our subjects allows us to subtly mirror them. It's better to adopt this stance as we respond in speech, and not to be too obvious. Just try matching someone's breathing some time and see what happens.

Psychological Rapport

On a psychological level, people tend to hear according to their personality types. If we take the simplified personality types such as **shark, whale, dolphin and urchin**, each has a different response to pace and engagement concerns.

Chapter 10

Four Personalities

Personality Styles

According to the direct sales arena, there are four major personality types\: The Shark, Whale, Sea Urchin, and Dolphin. People usually have all four types represented in their personality, but the percentage of each component typically varies. The Shark personality for instance, is usually fast-paced. You can hear it when they speak and see it when they walk. The urchin and shark are more fact-based. The other two relate more to emotion.

Sharks are people who tend to be flashier dressers. They like loud, bold colors such as green, red, blue, and orange. They like fancy cars, houses, and all the things money can buy. Sharks tend to talk a lot, and they tend to talk louder than everyone else. A shark has several mottos ("Winning isn't everything, it's the ONLY thing!" "I want it done, yesterday!"). People tend to buy into Sharks with no problem.

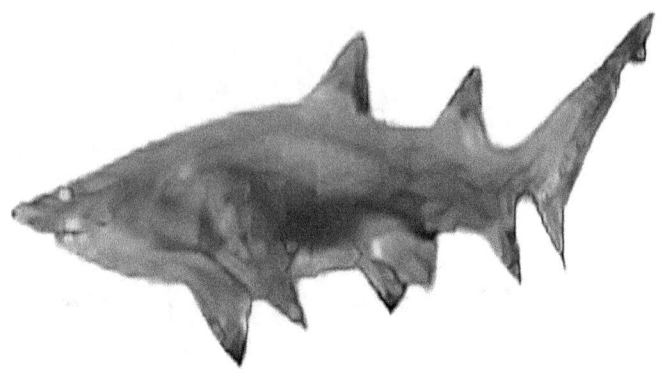

Sharks typically are not the best listeners. Sharks' strengths are: They're confident (sometimes too confident); they're also task-oriented and good salespeople. Their weaknesses are: they are impatient, competitive, and formal. A good example of a shark would be John Luke Picard from Star Trek. If you aren't yet 100% clear on what a shark is like, watch Star Trek. Sharks prefer succinct details and value results. They're also interested in **TASKS** and **OUTCOMES** – not people or relationships.

- They appear Competitive, Independent, Uncommunicative, and Formal.

- Their time has HIGH VALUE. They have low tolerance for wasting time or small talk.

- They expect you to stick to a schedule – respect their time – deliver as promised.

- They are annoyed by delays – lack of focus – poor results – indecisions – lollygagging – or failure to deliver.

- Sharks enjoy taking risks. When they make decisions, they place more stock in people who seem to be super-successful.

- Sharks move rapidly, always moving on to the next big idea.

Use this page to make some notes.

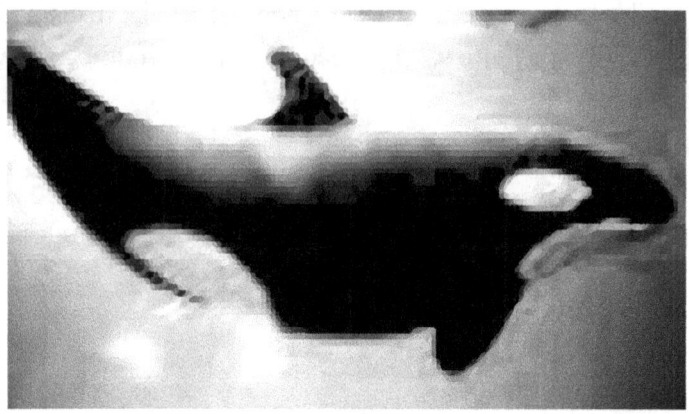

Whales are slower and will not follow a fast-paced presentation as well; they're also sometimes slow to make decisions. They are the individuals who would like everyone to get along. People tend to buy into them, because they are team players. Whales love to help people in need. They have several weaknesses as well, such as: they avoid confrontations and cannot handle pressure well. Two great examples of Whales are Princess Diana and Mother Teresa. Whales are some of the friendliest people that you can meet: They'll agree with you even when you're wrong!

- Whales want to control their environment.

- Whales want to know the outcome for every option.

- Whales tend to focus on productivity goals and efficiency, rather than devoting time and attention to casual relationships.

Chapter 10: Four Personalities

Dolphins will relate to fun and excitement and whales to helping people and contribution. Sharks respond to elements of power and control (they like things – fine cars, houses etc). Dolphins love fun and recognition, while whales need support and teamwork. Dolphins like to have <u>extra time</u> to make decisions and they avoid <u>Direct Confrontation</u>…thus it becomes tempting to attempt to exert yourself in order to achieve your objectives…however, this is rarely the best approach, as they may appear to be agreeing with you when, in fact, they do not.

Dolphins' annoyances are: Conflict – Gossip – Hurtful Behavior – Apathy – Pressure. Dolphin's strengths' are: they're competitive, demonstrative, and engaging. Their weaknesses are: They lose track of time, dislike details, are hard to commit, and they won't stay focused long. You're often more likely to be correct in assessing what personality type people are <u>not,</u> than exactly what they <u>are.</u> But this can narrow the field down quite quickly. Chris Rock and Jay Leno are good examples of Dolphins.

Chapter 10: Four Personalities

- Dolphins like to be managed through close relationships rather than by force.

- Most Dolphins appear nice, friendly, and comical.

- Dolphins are the most people-oriented of all of the personality types.

- Dolphins can typically get along with any personality.

Takes some notes about this personality.

Urchins value respect and making the right decisions. They're the people who want the facts and the statistics. If they decide to purchase a vehicle, expect them to need every single fact. When closing the deal, they will read the entire contract before signing. Urchins can easily be referred to as the people who are skeptical of everyone. You probably know some people who question everyone they come in contact with. Urchins are planners, organizers and they are very structured. Some of the Urchins' weaknesses are: They're sometimes aloof, cautious, and distant. Their strengths are: they're independent, can stay focused on a task for long periods of time. Urchins are Distant – Independent – take Extra Time – Aloof.

- Cooperative as long as they have some freedom to organize their own efforts.

- Tend to be Cautious about friendships or personal warmth.

- Often take their time to make decisions…you need to be patient.

- They tend to get irritated if they think you are using social skills or personality in lieu of competence.

- Value <u>Data and Facts</u> over charm and polish.

Annoyances include: Pressure – Inconsistency – Silliness – Neglect – Lack of facts – Erratic behavior – Ambiguity.

- Urchins want to know the facts.

- Most Urchins are compliant if they have the ability to have some freedom to make decisions.

- Urchins are careful and reserved, but once they establish trust they become dedicated and loyal.

To be more informed about personality characteristics, take a moment to figure out which fish fits your personality. What you will find out is that you have some traits of each fish, but more of others. Ask yourself who you know that displays some of these characteristics? When you can understand your personality better, then you can buy into yourself.

You are the product, since you are going to get people buying into you. With that being said, you need to find out who you are and what you have to offer. Your success or your failure during the interview process depends on whether you can answer the question of who you are. The sad part of the process is that most people think that they can just wing it through the interviewing process (wrong). I used to try and wing it through the interviews and realized quickly that I needed to practice. Some people say that practice makes perfect. I'm not buying into that, however, because I believe practice makes you better – but not perfect.

Chapter 11

Interviewing Skills

INTERVIEWING MADE EASY

Overview

A. 50% of a successful interview is enthusiasm, excitement & energy.

1. Introduce yourself (first & last name) to the receptionist or front desk. Let them know you have a scheduled interview with _____.

2. Bring multiple copies of your resume to hand to the interviewer when you reach the meeting room or their office.

3. Smile and build rapport with the interviewer.

4. Stay positive even if a current or past employer has not been your best experience.

5. Use eye contact.

6. BE PREPARED – look up the website. Know facts about the company and KNOW WHY YOU WOULD

WANT TO WORK IN THAT INDUSTRY AND THAT COMPANY!

B. 25% of the interview is selling yourself.

1. Know the entire sales process. Both parties should ask questions, probe for needs (Is your experience/personality what the company is looking for? DOES the industry/company offer the career growth/stability/environment/commission structure you're looking for?

2. Use your 3 MOST compelling success stories to illustrate your strengths.

3. Complete the FEB selling exercise.

C. 25% of the interview is the close.

1. The interview is a sales call. Your objective is to set up the next interview or get the job offer.

2. Ask lead-in questions to close the interviewer to set up the next interview, or to offer the position.

3. Overcome objections until you set up the next step or get the interviewer's recommendation.

4. Ask for the interviewer's business card (make sure their email and/or fax number is on it).

D. HAVE FUN!

For a phone interview:

Chapter 11: Interviewing Skills

- Stand up during the interview vs. sitting down.

- Have a glass of water nearby, just in case.

- Have your resume in front of you (highlight your best accomplishments - it will make you remember key selling points / strengths about yourself).

- Ask the interviewer for their email address so that you can send a thank you follow-up letter.

- CLOSE for a face-to-face meeting.

- If the interviewer is not the decision maker, ASK FOR THEIR RECOMMENDATION to whoever is the decision maker.

- Be prepared – know why you want to work in the industry and for the company (think of 3 reasons for each).

- Make sure all distractions are eliminated! (NO I pads, cell phones, pets, radios, TV's etc).

DO'S & DON'TS OF INTERVIEWING

Before the interview

DO dress in a business suit.

DO research the company.

DO examine sales books in order to brush up on the industry

DO arrive 10-15 minutes before an interview.

DO bring a copy of your resume.

DO prepare a copy of references.

DO bring a pen and notebook to takes notes before, during and after the interview.

DO prepare questions to ask during the interview.

DO greet everyone in the office with a smile and hello.

DO fill out all applications neatly and completely.

DO greet the interviewer with a smile and by his/her surname.

DO give a firm handshake.

DO make direct eye contact.

DO psych yourself up! It's OK if you are nervous or a little frightened. You have nothing to lose and everything to gain.

DON'T be unprepared for the interview. You'll never get a second chance to make a first impression.

During The Interview

DO demonstrate passion, enthusiasm and energy throughout the interview.

DO be yourself. People can tell when you're faking it.

DO be confident. You're the kind of employee this employer needs.

DO represent yourself honestly.

DO maintain direct eye contact.

DO sit up straight.

DO use FEB selling to answer the employer's questions.

DO ask questions about the position, company and the interviewer.

DON'T ask questions about salary, commission, bonuses, vacations or anything else the company can do for you. Wait until you've gotten the job offer.

DON'T get too comfortable. Remain professional and on guard.

DON'T ever say anything negative. Be careful when talking about past and present employers.

After The Interview

DO jot down notes to help you remember the highlights of the interview (questions, your impressions, your performance). This will help you in future interviews and writing thank you letters.

DO fax, email or drop off a thank you letter within 24 hours.

The "*Tell ME about Yourself*" Trap Question

Studies have found that in over 70% of initial interviews, interviewers will start the interview by asking: "Tell Me about yourself." Easy enough, right? Think again. This question alone can determine whether or not an interviewer decides to continue with the interview. Below is a list of questions that, once answered, will help provide a skeleton for your 2-minute "Tell Me About Yourself" pitch on yourself.

A. Questions to answer if you have less than 5 years of sales experience:

Why did you pick your University?

What types of activities were you involved in?

Did you participate in any leadership activities? If yes, what did you learn through them?

Were you involved in any internships? If yes, how competitive were they to get?

What did you learn through them?

How long did it take you to complete college?

Did you finance any of your education?

What achievement throughout college are you the most proud of?

How did you come to learn that Sales was the "right" career path for you?

For each sales position you have had, answer the following questions:

    Why did I choose to work there?

    What was I selling?

    Who was I selling to?

How is that position parallel to this position I am interviewing for?

How did I know I was doing well (think % of quota attainment, size of accounts you generated, awards, overall sales ranking)?

What 3 sales achievements am I the most proud of?

Why did I leave, or why am I looking to leave?

Is there anything about your former experience or anything reflected on your resume that you feel an employer might be concerned about? How are you prepared to address this concern?

What makes you qualified for the position you are interviewing with?

Why are you excited about the specific position and company that you are interviewing with?

B. Questions to answer if you have more than 5 years of sales experience:

How did you come to learn that Sales was the "right" career path for you?

For each sales position within the last 10 years, answer the following questions:

Why did I choose to work there?

What was I selling?

Who was I selling to?

How did I know I was doing well (think % of quota attainment, size of accounts you generated, awards, overall sales ranking)?

How was this sales job parallel to the position I am interviewing for?

What 3 sales achievements am I the most proud of?

Why did I leave or why am I looking to leave?

Is there anything about your former experience or anything reflected on your resume that you feel an employer might be concerned about? How are you prepared to address this concern?

What makes you qualified for the position you are interviewing for?

Why are you excited about the specific position and company that you are interviewing with?

SALES PROCESS

1. Identify Prospect – Make a plan, identify your target!

2. Build Rapport – firm handshake, good eye contact, build trust and credibility

3. Probe for needs (open vs. closed-ended questions)

4. Sell to Needs (Feature Example Benefit presentation)

5. Trial Close (Take their temperature/tie downs)

   "If we can provide you with ____, would you be ready to get started today?"

6. Seek out and Overcome Objections - hear it out/cushion or empathize/show them different route to getting what they want

7. Close – get hired or at least, set the next appt.

8. Recommendation/Referrals/Repeat Business

FEB SELL YOURSELF

During the interview it is essential that you SELL YOURSELF. Feature-Example-Benefit Selling, also known as FEB selling, is a fabulous way to do this! FEB selling teaches you to effectively sell yourself by using personal examples.

FEATURE: a fact that sets you apart from other people.

EXAMPLE: a specific, personal example that supports your fact.

BENEFIT: how your fact and example benefit the employer.

For example: *Feature-* strong work ethic

Example- while attending college full-time, I worked 40 hours a week to finance my education.

Benefit- I'm used to working hard in order to achieve positive results.

By using the examples above, we come up with this statement:

I have a strong work ethic. For example, while attending college full-time, I worked 40 hours a week to finance my education. What this means for XYZ Company is that I'm used to working hard in order to achieve positive results.

Below are some additional *features* many employers look for in their candidates. Examine your background and complete the *Example* and B *benefit column.*

FEATURE	EXAMPLE	BENEFIT
Aggressive		
Goal Oriented		
Motivated		
Resilient		
Persistent		

QUESTIONS COMMONLY ASKED

Most of us make two mistakes when we are being questioned in an interview. First, we fail to listen to the question. We proceed to answer a question that was not asked, or to give out a lot of superfluous information. Second, we attempt to answer questions without preparation. Not even the most skilled debater can answer questions off the cuff without damaging his or her chances of success. Bottom line...*BE PREPARED!*

1. Tell me about yourself.
2. What is your greatest strength?
3. What is your biggest weakness?
4. What are you looking for in a position?
5. What do you know about our company?
6. Why do you want to work for us?
7. Why do you want to work in this industry?
8. Why do you want sales?
9. What motivates you?
10. Why should we hire you? What sets you apart from others?
11. What qualities do you think a top sales representative possesses?
12. Why are you leaving your current company? Past companies?

13. Where else are you interviewing?
14. What is your biggest achievement?
15. What is your biggest failure? What did you learn from it?
16. Why did you select your college or university?
17. What motivated you to choose your major?
18. What are your goals over the next 3 years? 5 years? 10 years?
19. What do you see yourself doing in 5 years? What position do you see yourself in?
20. How much money do you want to make this year? 3 years? 5 years?
21. In your current or past positions, what features did you like the most? Least?
22. What would be your ideal job?
23. If you had your choice of companies, where would you go?
24. How do you define success?
25. What do you think it takes to be successful in our company?
26. How do you spend your spare time?
27. What books have you read recently?
28. Will you relocate? Does relocation bother you?
29. How do you think those that know you describe you?

30. Give an example of a time you had a conflict with a co-worker and how you handled it.
31. Did you ever work for a manager you didn't care for? What did you do about it?
32. Describe the relationship that should exist between a supervisor and sub-ordinates.
33. Give me a specific example of a time when you dealt with a disgruntled customer.
34. Tell me about an important goal you set for yourself in the past and how you achieved it.
35. Give me an example of a particularly difficult occasion when you had to be persuasive in order to get your ideas across.
36. Tell me about a time when you worked really hard for something over a period of time and did not get it.

SITUATIONAL QUESTIONS

Be sure to use the STAR format when answering any situational questions!! Be sure when answering interview questions that the answers are concise and specific.

S: Situation at hand
T: Task to resolve
A: Actions you took – 3 or 4 action item examples of what led to….
R: Result

RAPPORT BUILDING:

A demonstrated ability to establish and maintain positive working relationships with customers. An individual who communicates with others, building trust and credibility.

Please describe a time when you had to build rapport with a customer or co-worker in a particularly difficult situation.

Follow-up Questions:
Who was the customer or co-worker?

When did you do this?

Why was it particularly difficult for you?

What did you do to build rapport?

What were the results?

Can you tell me about a specific time that was important for you to build trust and credibility with another person? How did you do that?

Follow-up Questions:
Who was the person you needed to build trust and credibility with?

Why was that so important?

What did you do to attain that?

What was the outcome?

SALES APTITUDE/PERSUASIVENESS:

A demonstrated ability to persuade others to take action in a specific direction.

Please give me an example of a particularly difficult time when you had to be persuasive in order to get your ideas across.

Follow-up Questions:
What was the situation?

Why was it difficult?

What were you trying to accomplish?

What specific steps did you take to be persuasive? What were the results?

Please give me an example of a time when you were having difficulty closing a customer on your product or service.

Follow-up Questions:
Who was the customer?

When was this?

Why was it difficult?

What did you do to close the sale? Did you make the sale? What were the results?

PRO-ACTIVE/SELF-RELIANT:

A demonstrated ability to take action, being responsible for one's own success and failure. Take action to influence events and achieve specific goals. Demonstrates a willingness to originate actions.

Please tell me about an important goal you set for yourself in the past and how you achieved it.

Follow-up Questions:
Why was the goal important to you?

What steps did you take to achieve it?

What obstacles did you encounter along the way?

How did you overcome them?

What was the result?

Follow-up Questions:
Did you initiate any new procedures or systems?

How did you go about getting them improved?

Are they still being used?

How did they increase your effectiveness?

RESILIENCE:

A demonstrated ability to stick with a goal or desired result when faced with rejection or opposition. Maintain a positive attitude and work through obstacles.

Tell me about a time when you worked really hard for something over time & did not get it.

Follow-up Questions:
What was your goal?

What effort did you put forth to get it?

What obstacles were in the way?

What obstacles get in your way of you doing your job at work? What do you do to overcome them?

Follow-up Questions:
How do you handle the obstacles?

Have you suggested doing anything differently?

Do these obstacles still exist?

COMMUNICATION SKILLS:

A demonstrated ability to present information in a clear, concise, well organized fashion. The ability to listen for an individual's needs and desires, and identify hidden objections.

Can you give me a specific example of a time when you dealt with a disgruntled customer?

Follow-up Questions:
Who was the customer?

When did it happen?

What were the circumstances?

What was the result?

Tell me about a time when you had a conflict or disagreement with someone at work. How did you handle it?

Follow-up Questions:
Who was the conflict with?

What was it in regard to?

How did you approach the person to resolve it?

RIDE ALONG/OBSERVATION INFORMATION

1. Remember that this is still a formal step in the interview process, and perhaps the most important. Be sure to take detailed notes throughout the day! The Rep is watching you and will report back to the Hiring Mgr. (Caution: Do Not be too casual with the rep and be sure to ask professional questions).

    - Great questions to ask: What do you like most about your position and the company? How did you get to your current level in the company? What new business sales strategy has worked best for you? What is an example of one of your best sales successes? MOST IMPORTANT: Can I count on your recommendation for the job?

    - Bad questions to ask: Is your job hard? What do you like least? How much money do you make now? What is your turnover rate? How much vacation time do you get?

2. Be professional in dress, speaking, body language and demeanor. Be attentive and eager, remembering to build rapport and ask a lot of questions.

3. Get involved! If the trainer or rep is moving equipment or doing a demonstration, roll up your sleeves and HELP!

    - Hint: You MUST act as if you are already a sales rep with the company!

Chapter 11: Interviewing Skills

4. Remember, the rep will go back with a recommendation on whether you will fit in with the company and do well in the industry.

5. Understand a negative interview! Many companies will have the rep sell negative on the position. For example:

    - cold call 100% of the day

    - tell you that you will work long hours, when normal hours actually apply

    - take you to all the difficult accounts

6. CLOSE!!! Thank them for their time. Leave the rep with this information:

    - You learned a lot and he/she was very informative

    - You would enjoy working with him / her in the future – get their business card.

    - You want the job and would they please recommend you for the position.

    - Always see the hiring manager after your ride to ask for the job!

** ALWAYS SELL ~ DON'T TELL **

CLOSING THE INTERVIEW

It's the winning score, the bottom line, the name of the game, the cutting edge, and the point of it all. If you haven't guessed, closing is the most important part of your entire interview. The following is a step-by-step guideline to get you through closing the interview. The interview is a sales call; you are the product. If you don't close the interviewer on you, how can you expect them to visualize you closing a prospect on their product or service?

Employers expect you to close. *Don't be surprised if they make it tough on you!*

After the interviewer has concluded his/her questions, you must proceed into your close.

1. Ask the employer questions.

2. Ask a lead-in question.

3. Overcome concerns/objections/hesitations.

4. Close for the next step/job.

Ask The Employer Questions

Choose 3-5 questions for your interview. These questions are guidelines. Use your own creativity. It is important to be yourself in an interview. Employers will quickly see through a memorized and over-rehearsed question. **Never ask a company about sick leave, paid vacations, holidays or other benefits that allow you to get away from work unless you are getting an offer.

Chapter 11: Interviewing Skills

- What has your career path been?
- What have you liked most about the company and what have you liked least about it?
- What expectations do you have for the company in the next 5 years? 10 years?
- What does the training program consist of?
- What are my opportunities for advancement?
- How are promotions evaluated?
- How is performance evaluated?
- What are your expectations of a new hire?
- What separates your top producer from everyone else?
- What is your competitive edge?
- What is your company doing to gain market share?
- What are your company's strengths and weaknesses?
- What is the territory currently producing?
- What goals do you have for the territory in the next 12 months? What do you think it will take to get the territory to those numbers?
- If you had to isolate 3 things that determine a person's success with your company, what would they be?

Ask A Lead-In Question

The purpose of a lead-in question is to identify whether you did your job of selling yourself in the interview. If asked properly, the lead-in question will pull out objections/hesitations the employer has about you filling the position. Choose one of the following questions, or create your own based on the examples given.

- How do you see me fitting in?
- How do I compare to other people you have hired?
- Describe to me your top sales person…Do you feel I have those same qualifications?
- Describe your ideal candidate…Do you see me as that type of person?
- Am I the kind of person you are looking for?
- Are there any concerns you have about me filling the position?
- Can I count on your recommendation for the next step?

Overcome Concerns/Objections/Hesitations

If after you've asked your lead-in question the employer has not set up the next step, or you are not filling out the new-hire paperwork, there is still work to be done. The employer may still have genuine concerns or may create concerns to see how you handle the situation. Use FEB selling to overcome the objections.

Chapter 11: Interviewing Skills

Keep going until you feel you have overcome all the hesitations the employer has…only then should you proceed to the next step.

Close For The Next Step/Job

Now you're in the home stretch. Consider yourself on 3rd base with bases loaded and up to bat at the same time. The good news is, you're almost done! The bad news is, this is the most important part. It is absolutely crucial you ask the following questions:

For initial interviews: *Where do we go from here? Can we set that up right now?*

For final interviews: *Where do we go from here? When can I start?*

Don't forget, just as you have practiced your close, the employer has spent many an hour thinking of ways to strike you out. Some "strike out" statements are:

- I still have more people to interview.
- I will be getting back with your recruiter.
- I will be letting you know in a couple of days.

Beware of those smokescreens. DO NOT be fooled into thinking you will get the next step. If you don't set up the day, date and time of your next interview, it probably will never happen.

As a rule of thumb, attempt to get the next step 3 times. You may have to refer back to overcoming objections/concerns/hesitations to achieve this goal.

*As with everything, there may be an exception to the rule. For some unknown reason, the interviewer may not have the power to set up the next step. At least find out if the interviewer will be recommending you for the next step.

Writing A Thank You Letter- That Sells!!!

A thank-you letter should be more than a polite thank-you. Besides expressing interest in a position, thank-you letters can reinforce, correct a first impression or build on the relationship you've already established with the interviewer. Your thank-you letter should be emailed, faxed or dropped off within 24 hours of your interview. Don't delay!

The letter should be in a professional, business format.

1. Tell the interviewer how much you enjoyed meeting him or her.

2. Express your enthusiasm for the company and position.

3. Reiterate a specific selling point that was discussed in the interview.

4. Establish your next point of contact.

Remember: it's very important to sound genuine and sincere, and that requires a personal touch.

Chapter 12

Resume Information

New to the Industry:

If you do not have previous experience in the industry, the most important thing to know is that you will want to be sure you know EXACTLY what is expected of a rep. Below are some suggestions on helping to gain that knowledge:

What information should you know about yourself?

Since no one knows you better than yourself, you have to make them buy into you. The first thing you need to do is to interrogate yourself. Take a few sheets of paper and write the important points about yourself. Below are some suggestions for topics to put on your list. Once you have this information in place, it will be easier for you to deliver your benefits to the person who is interviewing you.

Honors and Awards

You should list all the honors and rewards you've received from past employers, community groups, churches, and schools. You may include testimonials from people that have helped you along the way.

Employment Information

This information is probably the most important, because potential employers want to know about your work history. You should write down all of the jobs you've ever held. Whether it was an internship, a part-time or full-time job, you need to write it down. You may, however, choose to leave an employer off the list if you got fired from that job. Under each job you should list the following items:

- The name of the past employer, telephone, address
- The dates you were employed there
- The name of your immediate supervisor

For each job, make sure you list the following:
- Key accolades that you received
- Your responsibilities and required duties
- If you received a promotion
- Skills that you gained from the job
- What you liked about the job and what you learned
- How many hours you worked per week

Responsibilities:

You should describe your responsibilities in three complete sentences. Here are a couple of examples of what yours could look like:

- Specific duties were to build and maintain 250 affluent accounts that were worth 5 million dollars.

- Sold phone services to new clients over the phone

Skills:
Make a list of the skills that were required to perform your duties, and also talk about what you developed. Below are a couple examples:

- Trained new hires on product and services

- Handled a book of business of 300 customers

Major accomplishments:
This is a great opportunity for you to brag on yourself. If you are going to brag, then make sure you can show results. Here are a couple of examples.

- Was the Number One sales representative within the company for 8 months in a row

- Grew the company share by 15 percent in 2010

Volunteer Work:
If you have participated in any volunteer programs, don't hesitate to list any of the organizations. For each, list the following:

- Name of your manager, or President of the organization

- Your name, email address, telephone number
- List dates that you volunteered
- If you have any recommendations that would be great, as well

Extracurricular Activities:
List any activities that you participated in. Under each you probably want to list the following:

- The name of the organization and the purpose of your being involved
- Any responsibilities that you held
- Accolades that you received
- Any key accomplishments

Chapter 13

Top Questions

Here are the Top 17 Questions and how to answer them:

1. Tell me about yourself!

When you're asked this question, please be careful how you answer, because it could make you or destroy your interview. There are two main reasons why people ask this question – usually asked at the beginning of the interview after some small talk:

- They think the interview should be a test, and they want to put you in the hot seat
- They've read the question in a book and want to try it out on you

Understanding how to respond is critical, and doing so within a minute or less vital. If you take more than a minute to respond, you could come across as boring. Therefore, you should take time to prepare a script on how you will answer this question. Here's a sample script to get you started:

Example Answer: Since you already have a copy of my resume explaining my work history, I believe you'll agree that I'm a good person with a good track record of success. I'm thinking that you might be looking for more than just a "good fit" to fill this position. After researching this position, I'm guessing you might be looking for some of the intangibles that wouldn't necessarily show up as specific line items on a resume.

For example, I'm thinking you might be looking for someone who can adjust fast and produce results quickly. You may also be looking for someone who can blend with the existing culture, but can still bring new ideas from outside the company. You might also be looking for someone who can grow the existing opportunities, while being able to defuse potential hot spots that may exist within problem customer accounts. If so, those are the types of things that have enabled me to be successful throughout my career.

Do you mind if I ask, what other goals would you want the perfect candidate for the position to be able to accomplish?

At this point in the conversation, the interviewer's decision-making process should be over, as he or she would likely be jumping up and down in their chair if someone showed up and demonstrated exactly what they were looking for.

For a career change-no job change, or new to the market
Example Answer: After beginning a career with [name of organization] as sales person and climbing the career ladder there, I accepted a position with [organization]. I am looking for a position with you because they have closed that location.

Chapter 13: Top Questions

2. **Why do you want to work in this type of industry?**

Example Answer: I have always wanted to work in an industry that_____. One of my passions is _____ projects, so I have collected a number of_____ from your company. I could be an _____ anywhere, but I would like to be employed by a company that I trust.

The Why: You should tell a story about how you got interested in this type of position. Make a comparison of the job you are currently interviewing for and your current position. Let your passion for your work become a theme that you refer back to throughout the interview.

3. What is your Dream Job?

This question gives you the opportunity to sell the interviewer on your skills that fit into the job description. Display an interest in showing how your skills can be put to use in the new job. Try to tie in the size of the company, the position, and other factors that are appropriate.

Example Answer: My dream job would include all of the duties and responsibilities that are required to do the job for the position that you're trying to fill. I thrive in fast-paced environments where growth is necessary. The job description said that you are looking for a person who has great oratorical skills. I feel that I possess those skills that you're looking for.

4. Why should I hire you?

This is one of the oldest questions in the book, so make sure you are prepared for it. Make sure you don't repeat your employment history or what's on your resume. Instead, offer one or two options to explain why you're interviewing with this company. The recruiter wants to know what you believe is your most compelling quality – the one that would make you stand out from all the other candidates.

Example Answer: I have a good friend who worked in this industry for several years. I had the opportunity to ask him about it and also to shadow him for a few hours on the job. For that reason, I believe I have a great understanding of how the business runs

_____

_____

_____

_____

_____

5. What are your strengths?

With this question you need to describe two or three skills that are most relevant for the job. Avoid things that are clichés or generalities; instead, use specific stories. Describe how your skills can be put to use for this current position.

Example Answer: My greatest strength is my public speaking skills; I can usually win people over to my point of view. I also have great decision-making skills under pressure. These skills seem to be directly related to this job. I noticed that you require ____ amount of years of experience. I know that my resume shows only 2 years of experience, but it doesn't show that I took several classes related to this job. I also make it a common practice to read magazines in order to gain insight into this field. I'm sure that this combination of knowledge and skill level is equivalent to that of people who have three years of experience. As a matter of fact, I'm currently enrolled in a public speaking course where I can see results already.

6. **Considering your resume, what are your weaknesses in relation to this job?**

The best approach is maybe to redirect the question back to the interviewer to see what he or she thinks the weaknesses are. Once they respond, you now have the opportunity to change their mind with examples.

Example Answer: What are you most concerned about? If it's my experience, I can assure you that my public speaking, people skills, and decision-making skills qualify me for this job.

7. **Tell me about a time when you had to deal with an upset customer. How did you handle the customer?**

This question is a situational question, which you should answer using the STAR method that we have talked about. The interviewer wants to see how you react when you're under fire from your customers. Make sure that your answer talks about the situation, task, action that you took, and the results.

Example Answer: I was working in my office one day when I heard three hard knocks. So I opened the door and it was one of my customers, Mr. Rodgers. His **situation** was that he had just closed a loan with me two days ago, but he received a phone call from another bank stating that he could get a better rate. My **task** was to sell Mr. Rodgers on why he should not refinance his loan with the other bank. The **action** I took was to invite Mr. Rodgers to meet with me and to show him the advantages and disadvantages of doing business with me as opposed to the other bank. As a **result** of my showing him how all of the advantages outweighed the disadvantages, he became one of my longtime customers. I have since been able to handle other loans for him and his friends.

8. Describe your ideal career.

When answering this question you should talk about your passions, skills, and what comes natural to you. Talk about what you expect to learn in this new position. Try not to mention specific time frames because this may give the impression that you are a job hopper.

Example Answer: I would prefer to stay in a career related to selling and public speaking. I am also interested in how businesses run; however, I really feel like education would be something that I would like to do long term.

9. Tell me what you know about our company.

This has to be one of the oldest interviewing questions. It gives you the opportunity to let the interviewer know that you've done extensive research on the company. Try to describe the product and services that the company offers and show how they line up with your goals. You should also describe what would be motivating to you about working for this company.

Example Answer: I served as a summer intern for your company last summer, so I was able to follow your business model. After observing first-hand your business model, – in a nutshell, integrity – I decided that I would like to work for your company long term.

10. How do you handle pressure from your boss?

The best way or the safest way to answer this question is to try and explain an example of miscommunication. The person interviewing will want to know how you would prevent the situation from reoccurring in the future.

Example Answer: The only situation of this nature that I can remember was when my boss and I got too busy to keep each other informed. He over-committed me, by scheduling me for a presentation which I was not available for because I had to present to another client. From then on, we both always check one another's calendar before making a commitment.

11. Tell me about a time when you got frustrated at work.

This is a question designed to see what type of personality you have. Most interviewers want to make sure that you can handle yourself under pressure.

Example Answer: I was frustrated that one of my clients wanted to cancel a loan that he had just signed. He said that an opposing bank offered him a better rate. I had a hard time convincing him otherwise, but I persisted, and after showing him how his relationships with our bank benefited him, he decided to keep the loan.

12. How long do you plan to work for our company?

This question is similar to "Where do you see yourself in five years?" When answering, you need to be specific and talk about the position that you would hold. You may want to include a comment about wanting to get promoted to the next position.

Example Answer: I would like to grow, learn new skills, and achieve new levels in this position. As long as I consider myself growing and contributing to the company, it will make sense for me to continue with the company.

13. **If you are not at work, do you like to be on a schedule or do you like to be spontaneous?**

   When you answer this question, you need to make sure that it lines up with the type of job you are interviewing. For example if you're applying for a sales job, you may want to answer that you prefer being spontaneous, like rejection, and are persistent. Remember that this question is about your personality and compatibility with the job.

   Example Answer: My workdays are scheduled in advance, because I have several meetings a day. On the weekends I have plans, but not a set schedule. I find this is a good way to relax.

14. Did your customers enjoy working with you?

To answer this question, you need to talk about having repeat customers, why your clients preferred you, and how you kept their business. You could use a story about one of your difficult customers whose business you gained for life.

Example Answer: My client enjoyed working with me, because when he was in my office I focused all of my attention on him. If a client was in my office, I made him feel like he was the only thing that existed for that moment.

15. What motivates and excites you?

Tell the interviewer about your hobbies or strengths as they relate to the position you are interviewing for.

Example Answer: The opportunity to work for a Fortune 500 company, where I will have the chance to help, save, and empower lives.

16. How do you stay current with industry news?

The interviewer wants to know that you have a zest for the industry. They also want to know that you do your research.

Example Answer. I usually read the NY Times, Wall Street Journal, and the (name of the major local newspaper of the city/town where the company is located). I also subscribe to several newsletters, which keeps me informed about the new trends.

17. Tell about an organization that you participated in outside of work that benefited you.

When answering this question you need to discuss in detail your intiative: perhaps something you volunteered for, held leadership positions in, and/or an organization that you gained skills from.

Example answer: I recently joined a toastmasters class to further develop my public speaking skills.

Chapter 14

Conclusion

Well hopefully you have learned all about what it takes to get people to buy into you. Remember that people know you, like you, and trust you for several reasons. Be certain to routinely review the principles in this book over the next few years of your life- each day you mature. Its been my pleasure to deliver this information to you.

Remember: "The person who really wants to do something finds a way; the other person finds an excuse"

Bibliography

Carnegie, Dale. How to Win Friends and Influence People. 1936. Revised edition. New York: Pocket Books, 1981

Cooper, Robert. The Other 90%. New York: Three Rivers Press, 2001

Coore-Hershkowitz, Sue. How To Say It To Sell It. New York: Prentice Hall Press, 2008

Covey, Stephen. The 7 Habits of Highly Effective People. New York: 1989

Fraser, George. Click. New York: McGraw Hill 2008

Gitomer Jeffrey. Little Red Book of Selling. Austin: Bard Press, 2005

Hogan, Kevin. The Psychology of Persuasion. Gretna, Louisiana: Pelican Publishing, 1996

Maxwell, John. The 21 Irrefutable Laws Of Leadership. Nashville, TN: Thomas Nelson Publishers, 1998

Pincus, Marilyn. Get The Job! Interview Strategies That Work. New York: Main Street Books, 1999

Simmons, Annette. The Story Factor. New York: Perseus Books Group 2001

Willingham Ron. Integrity Selling. New York: 1987

Treandos Thornton

Youth & College Speaker
**Author of
"Get Them to
   Buy Into YOU"**

The Student Guide to
Personal & Professional Success

Treandos Thornton is a powerful speaker, entrepreneur, and a member of
KAPPA ALPHA PSI. At the age of 22, Treandos graduated at the top of his class with a degree in Business Management from Valdosta State University Business School. Treandos has read over 150 books on personal development. He has spent over a decade in the sales industry and has been named is the #1 Sales Consultant in multiple organizations.
Book Treandos today:

www.treandos.com
www.treandosspeaks.com

www.ingramcontent.com/pod-product-compliance
Lightning Source LLC
LaVergne TN
LVHW051505070426
835507LV00022B/2942